DO STARS HAVE POINTS?

Questions and Answers About Stars and Planets

MELVIN AND GILDA BERGER

ILLUSTRATED BY VINCENT DI FATE

SCHOLASTIC REFERENCE

Contents

KEY TO ABBREVIATIONS

Measurements in metrics are in parenthesis.

g = gram
kg = kilogram
km = kilometer/kilometre
m = meter/metre
t = tonne
oC = degrees Celsius

For denominations more than one million, this book uses the word *billion* to mean 1,000,000,000 (10^9) and *trillion* to mean 1,000,000,000,000 (10^{12}).

Text copyright © 1998 by Melvin and Gilda Berger
Illustrations copyright © 1998 by Vincent Di Fate
All rights reserved. Published by Scholastic Inc.
SCHOLASTIC and associated logos are trademarks and/or registered trademarks of Scholastic Inc.

No part of this publication may be reproduced, or stored in a retrieval system, or transmitted in any form or by any means, electronic, mechanical, photocopying, recording, or otherwise, without written permission of the publisher. For information regarding permissions, write to Scholastic Inc., Attention: Permissions Department, 555 Broadway, New York, NY 10012.

Library of Congress Cataloging-in-Publication Data
Berger, Melvin
    Do stars have points? / Melvin and Gilda Berger.
             p.   cm.
    Summary: Questions and answers explore various aspects of stars
      and our solar system, including the sun, planets, moons, comets, and
      asteroids.
    1. Astronomy—Miscellanea—Juvenile literature. 2. Stars—Miscellanea—Juvenile litera-
    ture. 3. Solar system—Miscellanea—Juvenile literature. [1. Solar system—Miscellanea.
    2. Astronomy—Miscellanea. 3. Questions and answers.] I. Berger, Gilda. II. Title.
    QB46.B463   1998   523—DC21   97-36005   CIP   AC

ISBN 0-590-13080-3 (pob)
ISBN 0-439-08570-5 (pb)

Book design by David Saylor and Nancy Sabato

20 19 18 17 16 15 14 13   4 5 6 / 0

Printed in the U.S.A.   08
First printing, August 1999

Expert reader: Dr. Thomas Lesser, formerly Senior Lecturer, The American Museum-Hayden Planetarium

For Benny, a bright star in our constellation
— M. AND G. BERGER

For Ro, Chris, and Vic, of course, and for Chesley Bonestall who ignited the spark and for my dear friends Wayne Borlowe, Jeff Rovin, Bob Stephens, and Murray Tinkelman, who have kept that spark alive
— V. DI FATE

Introduction

Why read a question-and-answer book?

Because you're a kid! And kids are curious. It's natural—and important—to ask *questions* and look for *answers*. This book answers many questions that you may have:

- Where did the stars come from?
- How are planets different from stars?
- Why don't we feel Earth moving?
- Is there life elsewhere in the universe?

Many of the answers will surprise and amaze you. We hope they'll tickle your imagination. Maybe they'll lead to *more questions* calling for *more answers*. That's what being curious is all about.

Melvin Berger   *Gilda Berger*

STARS

Do stars have points?

No. Stars are huge, round balls of hot, glowing gas. They seem pointy to us because we see them through the moving layers of air and dust that surround Earth. The moving layers bend and break the starlight, making the stars look pointy.

The next time you take a bath or go swimming, look at your feet. Notice how the moving water breaks up the light and changes the shape of your toes. It's like the moving layers of air scattering the light from the stars.

How many stars can you see on a dark, clear night?

You can see about 3,000 stars with your eyes alone. But keep in mind that you are viewing only part of the sky. If the whole sky were visible, you could count about 5,000 stars.

If you look through a small telescope you might see as many as 600,000 stars. Through the most powerful telescope astronomers can spot *millions* of stars.

No one is sure exactly how many stars there are altogether. But astronomers believe there are at least 200 billion billion stars out in space!

Which is the brightest star in the night sky?

Sirius (SIHR-ce-us), sometimes called the Dog Star, is the brightest star that we can see. Although it is about the same size as the sun, Sirius is nearly 30 times brighter. Astronomers call it a star of the first magnitude—a measure of a star's brightness.

Sirius is a binary star because it has a smaller star circling around it. It takes about 50 years for the smaller star to make a complete turn around Sirius.

What are stars made of?

The stars are mostly hot gases. The chief gas is hydrogen (HYE-druh-juhn).

Hydrogen gas consists of tiny bits called atoms. The heat inside the stars makes the hydrogen atoms jump about. They keep on bumping into one another. Sometimes two hydrogen atoms bump so hard that they join together. The process is called nuclear fusion. This produces a tiny flash of light and a small burst of heat.

All of these collisions add up. Inside every star, hundreds of millions of tons of hydrogen atoms are joining together every second. The collisions shoot billions of flashes of light and bursts of heat out into space at the same time. And the collisions go on and on.

Where did the stars come from?

Astronomers think they know. Long, long ago, everything in the entire universe was scrunched tightly together into a small ball. Then, about 13 billion years ago, there was a huge explosion. Scientists call the explosion the Big Bang. They believe that the Big Bang was the birth of the universe.

The Big Bang sent gas and dust flying out into space. The gas and dust were made up of tiny bits of many different chemicals. Slowly they came together in giant clouds. Gravity pulled the clouds in together, tighter and tighter. In time, the force of gravity shaped the clouds into immense spheres.

At first, each sphere stretched across about 10 trillion miles (16 trillion km). Over millions of years, the spheres grew smaller and smaller. In time they were a million miles (1.6 million km) across. And that's when the first stars were born!

How did the solar system form?

Most scientists think the sun and planets were formed from a giant cloud of gas and dust about five billion years ago. The force of gravity pulled most of the gas and dust toward the center. This large mass became the sun. But clouds of gas and dust were left over. They continued to fly around the sun. Eventually, these clouds pulled together into much smaller balls that became the planets.

Are new stars forming today?

Yes. Plenty of gas and dust is still floating around in space. Some of it is left over from the Big Bang. Some comes from old stars that have exploded, hurling huge amounts of gas and dust out into space.

A new star begins when the clouds of gas and dust come together. When they get small enough, the gas gets hotter and hotter. The atoms bump and stick together, sending out tremendous amounts of heat and light. And new stars are created, just like the stars that formed after the Big Bang.

Do old stars die?

Indeed they do. Over billions of years, stars use up their hydrogen and get smaller. Some stars shrink and become so tiny that they are called white dwarfs. White dwarfs are very heavy. A teaspoon of a white dwarf weighs about 1,000 tons (1.016 t)!

Sometimes the white dwarf suddenly becomes much brighter. It turns into a nova. Sometimes the star explodes and is completely destroyed. Then it's called a supernova. The light from a supernova is a million times brighter than the light from a nova.

Stars may also shrink until they are only a few miles (kilometers) across. Then they can become black holes. The pull of gravity in a black hole is superpowerful. It is so strong that it does not even let light escape. Without light, the star is completely dark in the sky.

Which star is closest to Earth?

The sun. It is about 93 million miles (149 million km) from us. That makes it close enough to look like a round ball instead of a speck of starlight. It is also close enough for us to feel its tremendous heat and get its powerful light.

But don't think it's a quick trip to the sun. A car going 60 miles (96 km) an hour would reach the sun in 177 years. At 25,000 miles (40,000 km) an hour, it would take a rocket more than five months to cover the distance. Light from the sun, which speeds along at an incredible 186,000 miles (297,600 km) per second, takes just over eight minutes to reach Earth!

How hot is the sun?

Hotter than anything on Earth! The surface of the sun is about 10,000 degrees Fahrenheit (5,532 °C). The inside of the sun is even hotter. It's about 27 million degrees (13 million °C). Compare that to a gas kitchen stove, which only reaches 1,000 degrees (537 °C).

Only a small part of the sun's heat and light energy reaches Earth. Yet life on Earth depends on this energy. Plants need it to grow. Some animals eat the plants. Others eat the plant-eating animals. Life on Earth would be impossible without energy from the sun.

How do astronomers take a star's temperature?

They look at its color. As you know, things change color with heat. A piece of metal may be black. Heat it, and the metal becomes red hot. Make it even hotter, and it turns white hot.

A star's color tells the temperature at its surface. Red stars are coolest at about 5,000 degrees Fahrenheit (2,757 °C). Blue-white stars are hottest. They can reach 50,000 degrees (27,700 °C). The sun, a yellow star, is in between—10,000 degrees Fahrenheit (5,532 °C).

Astronomers also take a star's surface temperature by passing its light through a special glass called a prism. The prism breaks the light up into a series of colored lines. From these lines, scientists can find the star's exact temperature.

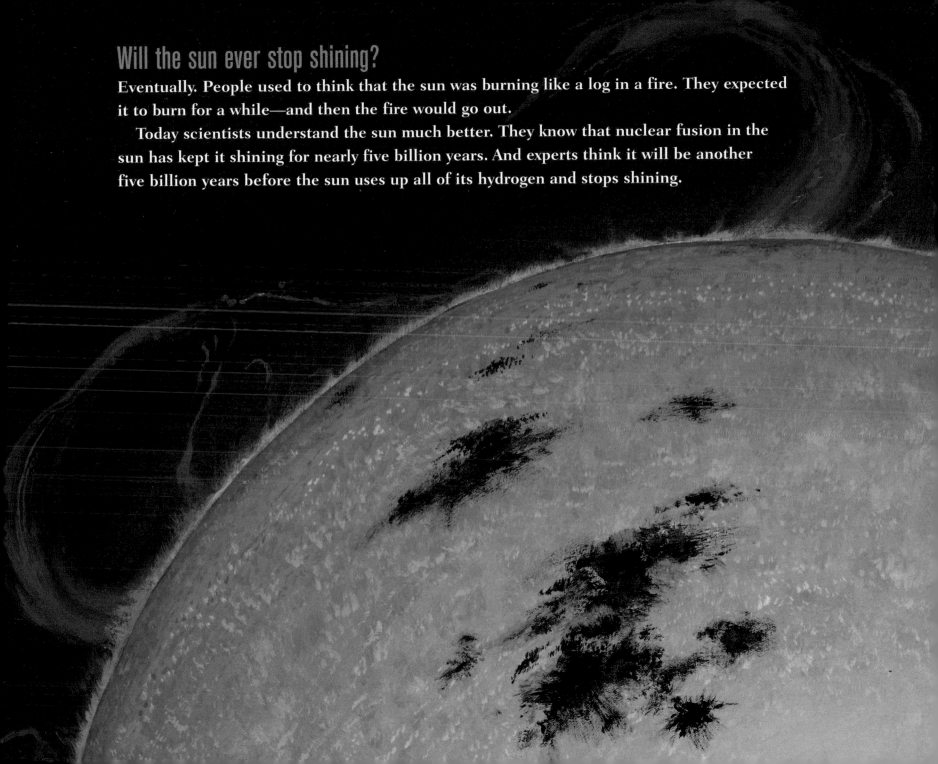

Will the sun ever stop shining?

Eventually. People used to think that the sun was burning like a log in a fire. They expected it to burn for a while—and then the fire would go out.

Today scientists understand the sun much better. They know that nuclear fusion in the sun has kept it shining for nearly five billion years. And experts think it will be another five billion years before the sun uses up all of its hydrogen and stops shining.

Which is bigger, the sun or Earth?

The sun is, by far. It is about 865,000 miles (1,384,000 km) across. That is, it has a diameter of 865,000 miles (1,384,000 km). In fact, the sun's diameter is over 100 times the diameter of Earth. The sun is so huge that more than one million Earths could easily fit inside it!

Suppose you were to draw the sun the size of a quarter. Then you would have to draw Earth the size of the period at the end of this sentence.

But the sun is not the biggest star. It is only a medium-sized star. The largest stars are more than 1,000 times the size of the sun. The smallest stars are even smaller than Earth.

Why do the other stars look so much smaller than the sun?

Because they are so far away. Proxima Centauri, the next nearest star to the sun, is 25 *trillion* miles (40 trillion km) away.

Light from Proxima Centauri takes more than four years to reach Earth. If you look at Proxima Centauri tonight, you will see light that left the star more than four years ago.

Imagine now that you have magic boots. With these boots you could reach the sun in one giant step. You would need another 300,000 giant steps to reach Proxima Centauri! And the other stars are many thousands of giant steps farther away.

Are the brightest stars always the largest stars?

Not at all. The brightness that we see depends on the amount of light energy the star sends out. A small, hot star sends out more light than a larger, cooler star. Take the stars named Rigel (RYE-gel) and Betelgeuse (BEE-tel-jooz), for example. Rigel is smaller than Betelgeuse. But Rigel sends out more light because it is a hotter star.

Also, how bright a star appears depends on how far the star is from Earth. Suppose there are two equally bright stars. One is close to Earth and one very far away. The closer star looks brighter than the star that is farther away.

Where are the stars during the day?

They're where they are at night—it's just that you can't see them. The sun's light is so bright that it blots out the dim light from the distant stars.

Something similar happens when you are watching a movie in a dark theater. If someone opens a door, a bright light floods the screen. It blots out the light from the movie projector. In the same way, the sun makes the sky too bright to see the stars during the day.

Why does the sun rise and set?

Actually, it doesn't! The sun always shines. It just *looks* as if it rises and sets every day.

Earth spins around, or rotates, all the time. When your part of Earth turns toward the sun, it seems to rise. When your part of Earth rotates away from the sun, it seems to set. The sun does not rise and set. It just looks that way because we are seeing the sun from a turning Earth.

Is each star alone in space?

No. Every star belongs to a large group of stars called a galaxy. Each galaxy has between a billion and a trillion stars. And there are about 50 billion galaxies throughout the universe. Our sun is part of a galaxy called the Milky Way. Astronomers say that the Milky Way galaxy contains 100 billion stars.

When you look up on a clear dark night, you can see part of the Milky Way. It is a band of hazy white light across the sky. To people long ago it looked like a splash of milk, so they named it the "Milky Way."

How big is the Milky Way galaxy?

Too big to be easily measured in miles (kilometers). Instead, astronomers measure the distance in light-years. A light-year is the distance that light, which moves at 186,000 miles (297,600 km) a second, travels in one year. A light-year is just less than 6 trillion miles (9.6 trillion km). The distance across the Milky Way galaxy is about 100,000 light-years—or 6 million billion miles (9.6 million billion km)!

Is the sun near the center of our galaxy?

No. The sun is off to one side.

Our galaxy is shaped like a gigantic pinwheel with a bulge in the center. The arms of the pinwheel extend out from the bulge. The sun is in one of the arms. It is about 33,000 light-years from the center.

The sun and all the stars are moving around the center of the galaxy. The sun travels at a speed of about 156 miles (250 km) a second. At that speed, it takes 250 million years for the sun to complete one giant loop around the Milky Way.

Andromeda galaxy

Can we see other galaxies besides the Milky Way?

We can see three other galaxies without a telescope. Each looks like a hazy patch of light in the night sky.

From the Northern Hemisphere we can see the Andromeda galaxy. It is 2,200,000 light-years away. Andromeda is even bigger than the Milky Way galaxy.

From the Southern Hemisphere we can see two galaxies called the Large and Small Magellanic Clouds. They are respectively 160,000 and 180,000 light-years from Earth.

Small Magellanic Cloud

Large Magellanic Cloud

How far is the most distant galaxy?

Scientists believe it is about 13 billion light-years away—a distance of 80,000,000,000,000,000,000,000 miles (128,000,000,000,000,000,000,000 km)! Some say this may be the edge of the universe. Others believe the universe may not even have a boundary.

Astronomers know that all the galaxies in the universe are rushing away from each other today. But no one knows if this will continue forever or if they will start coming together in time.

Is a constellation the same as a galaxy?

No. A constellation is a group of perhaps a dozen bright stars—and many more stars that are not as bright—all in the same area of the sky. A galaxy, you know, has billions of stars stretched over a much greater distance.

Long ago, people looked in wonder at the groups of stars that make up the constellations. In their minds they drew lines joining the stars—just like connect-the-dot puzzles—to make pictures in the sky. Some of the pictures were of legendary figures, such as Hercules and Pegasus. Others were of animals, such as Taurus the bull.

Astronomers have divided the sky into 88 constellations. They use them to locate objects in the night sky, just as you use addresses to locate houses. Constellations also help tell directions at night.

Are all the stars in a constellation the same distance from Earth?

Every star in a constellation is at a different distance from Earth. Some are closer; some are farther away. But as we look up, the points of light fool our eyes into believing that every star is the same distance from Earth.

Also, constellations are made up of stars of different brightnesses. Take Cygnus, the swan, for example. The star Deneb is a very bright star in the night sky. The rest of the swan is made up of fainter stars.

Do all people see the same constellations?

No. The constellations you can see will depend on where you live. Some constellations can only be seen in the Northern Hemisphere, others only in the Southern Hemisphere.

People who live on the equator are lucky. They can see all the constellations—but not all at once. It takes a whole year for all of the constellations to be visible from the equator.

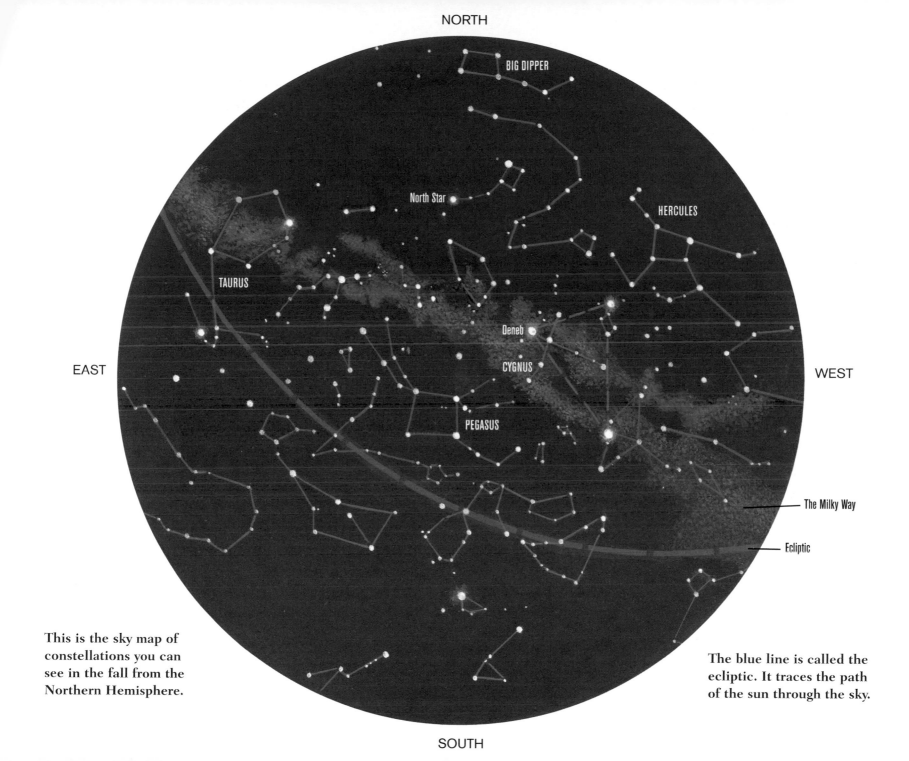

NORTH

BIG DIPPER

North Star

HERCULES

TAURUS

Deneb

EAST

CYGNUS

WEST

PEGASUS

The Milky Way

Ecliptic

This is the sky map of
constellations you can
see in the fall from the
Northern Hemisphere.

The blue line is called the
ecliptic. It traces the path
of the sun through the sky.

SOUTH

Is the Big Dipper a constellation?

Many people say it is. They're wrong!

The Big Dipper is only *part* of a constellation. It belongs to the constellation Ursa Major, or Great Bear. A group of stars within a constellation is called an asterism.

The Big Dipper asterism contains seven stars. They form a cup with a handle. The two stars of the front of the cup point to the North Star.

Why is the North Star important?

The North Star does not seem to move like the other stars. That's because it is almost straight up over the North Pole. From the Northern Hemisphere the North Star looks like it stays in one place.

Because the North Star seems fixed in the sky, sailors have long used it to help them find their way. The North Star is also called Polaris, or the polestar.

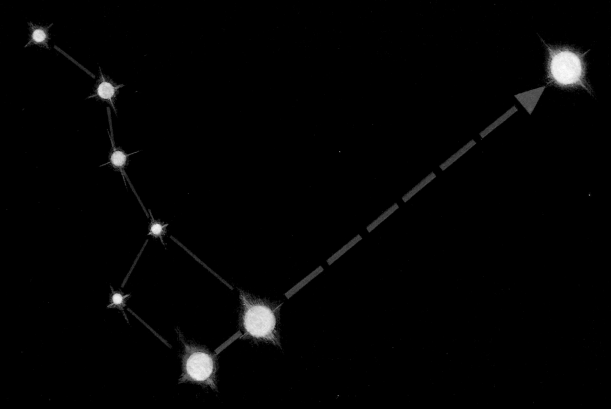

PLANETS

What are planets?

Planets are dark bodies that move around stars. Like stars, planets were formed from giant clouds of dust and gas.

Nine planets—Mercury, Venus, Earth, Mars, Jupiter, Saturn, Uranus, Neptune, and Pluto—spin around the sun. Together with the sun they make up our solar system. The sun is at the center. The nine planets and other bodies move in orbits around the sun.

How are planets different from stars?

Planets are much smaller than stars. The biggest planet is just one-tenth the size of the sun.

Planets weigh far less than stars. All the planets together weigh less than one-hundredth as much as the sun. Some planets are solid rock; some have solid centers covered by liquid and gas. Stars are balls of gases. Planets are dark and cold. We see them only because they reflect the sun's light. Nearly all of their heat energy comes from the sun.

Do planets and stars look alike?

Yes—but there are differences. Planets look like small, round disks. They shine with a steady light. Their light passes through a thick layer of moving air, which makes them look fuzzy around the edge. Stars look more like tiny points of light. They twinkle. Since they are so much farther away, their light sparkles and glitters.

Stars seem to be standing still. Planets change their position from night to night. That is why ancient Greeks named them planets, a word that means "wanderers." Today we know that the stars are also moving. But from Earth they look as if they are staying in one place.

Mercury

Venus

Earth

Mars

Jupiter

Do the planets move?

Indeed they do. The planets move in several ways. They revolve in giant loops around the sun. The path they follow is called an orbit. The farther the planet is from the sun, the longer it takes to orbit the sun. Mercury, the closest planet to the sun, takes about 88 days to make the journey. Pluto, the most distant planet, needs 91,000 days!

At the same time, each planet spins around, or rotates, on its axis. The axis is an imaginary line that runs from the North Pole to the South Pole. The time it takes to spin around once varies widely. Jupiter takes less than 10 hours. Venus takes 243 days.

Finally, the planets are moving through the Milky Way galaxy. They are traveling together with the sun around the center of the galaxy. It takes them about 250 million years to complete one loop.

Saturn

Uranus

Neptune

Pluto

Are the planets' orbits closer to the sun at some times and farther away at other times?

Yes. All planets are a little nearer to the sun at some times in their orbits than they are at other times. That's because the planets don't revolve in circles. They travel in oval-shaped, or elliptical, orbits.

Earth, for example, is about 91,400,000 miles (146,200,000 km) from the sun at the nearest point of its orbit, called perihelion (per-uh-HEE-lee-uhn). At the point farthest from the sun, called aphelion (uh-FEE-lee-uhn), Earth is 94,500,000 miles (151,200,000 km) away.

Do the planets sometimes speed up and sometimes slow down?

The nearer the planets are to the sun, the faster they move. The farther away they are, the slower they move.

When Earth is closer to the sun, it is winter in the Northern Hemisphere. The planet is moving faster. For that reason, fall and winter last only 179 days.

When Earth is farther away from the sun, it is summer in the Northern Hemisphere. Earth moves more slowly. Spring and summer last a full 7 days longer, or 186 days!

What makes the seasons on Earth?

The tilt of Earth. Half the year the Northern Hemisphere leans toward the sun. The sun's rays warm that part of the globe. It is spring and summer.

The rest of the year the Northern Hemisphere leans away from the sun. It gets less warmth from the sun. Then it's fall and winter in the Northern Hemisphere.

The Southern Hemisphere leans in the opposite direction. When it's summer in the Northern Hemisphere, it's winter in the Southern Hemisphere. And when it's winter in the Northern Hemisphere, it's summer in the Southern Hemisphere.

Do all parts of the globe have four seasons?

No. Around the equator, the climate is always warm. This part of the globe usually has just two seasons—rainy and dry.

The polar regions are always cold. They also have only two seasons—sunny and dark.

How fast is Earth moving?

Faster than you can imagine! Earth revolves around the sun at an average speed of 66,600 miles (106,560 km) an hour.

Earth also rotates. It takes 24 hours to make one complete turn. Of course, not all points on Earth move at the same speed. A point at the North Pole spins slowly in place. A point on the equator—which is 24,900 miles (40,000 km) long—speeds around at 1,038 miles (1,661 km) an hour!

At the same time, Earth, the sun, and the whole solar system revolve around the center of the galaxy. They race along at a speed of 560,000 miles (896,000 km) an hour.

Why don't we feel Earth moving?

Because everything on or near Earth is moving with us at the same time. We and the air around us are anchored to Earth by the force of gravity. So everything around us is revolving and rotating with planet Earth.

How big is Earth?

If you were to dig a hole straight down from the North Pole to the South Pole, you would dig for 7,900 miles (12,640 km) before reaching your goal.

But if you started your hole on the equator, you would have to dig farther. Earth is 7,927 miles (12,683 km) across at the equator.

There's a reason for this: Earth is not exactly round. You know that Earth is spinning very fast. This makes a slight bulge just below the equator. From space, Earth looks like a beach ball that's not fully blown up. It sticks out around its middle and is a little flatter on its top and bottom.

What is planet Earth made of?

The top part of Earth is its crust. It lies under the cities, farms, lakes, and oceans of the world. The crust is made up of 30 huge, separate, slow-moving plates of rock. The moving plates are from 5 to 25 miles (8 to 40 km) thick. They carry the land and oceans with them. Beneath Earth's crust is the 1,800-mile-deep (2880 km) mantle. It is made of very hot rock that ranges from about 1,600 degrees to 8,000 degrees Fahrenheit (871-4,426 °C).

Next is Earth's deeper outer core, made of melted iron and nickel. It is 1,400 miles (2,240 km) thick. Its temperature reaches 11,000 degrees Fahrenheit (6,087 °C). Finally, there is the inner core, which is solid iron and nickel and is 800 miles (1,280 km) across. Its temperature, which is hotter than the surface of the sun, tops 13,000 degrees Fahrenheit (7,200 °C).

No, it keeps changing. Some of the changes happen very fast. A volcano erupts and forms a mountain that looks like an upside-down ice-cream cone. An earthquake shakes the land and leaves a big gap on the surface.

Other changes are so slow that they are hard to notice. Mountains are slowly pushed up by movements in Earth's crust. Over millions of years, rivers cut giant canyons through the land. Wind and rain gradually wear away the tallest mountains.

29

Where does outer space begin?

About 60 miles (95 km) above Earth's surface. Beyond that the air that makes up our atmosphere becomes extremely thin. At a height of about 1,000 miles (1,600 km) the atmosphere ends. But outer space goes on and on.

What does Earth look like from space?

Astronauts see Earth as a blue-and-white ball. The blue is not the sky—it's Earth's oceans. About 70 percent of Earth's surface is covered with water. They also see small bits of land peeking out from behind the clouds.

The white is clouds that float in Earth's atmosphere. Clouds cover at least part of Earth all the time.

Who was the first human being in space?

Yuri Gagarin (1934–1968), a Russian cosmonaut, on April 12, 1961. He rocketed to a height of 203 miles (325 km). His spacecraft made one orbit of Earth at a speed of more than 17,000 miles (27,200 km) an hour for almost two hours.

Alan Shepard (1923–1998) was the first American astronaut to blast off from Earth. On May 5, 1961, his spacecraft, *Freedom 7*, rose to an altitude of 117 miles (187 km).

On which planet would you roast during the day and freeze at night?

Mercury. When the sun is shining, the temperature on Mercury reaches 800 degrees Fahrenheit (426 °C). But at night the temperature drops sharply to nearly –300 degrees (–184 °C). That's a difference of more than 1,100 degrees Fahrenheit (600 °C)! Mercury has no air around it. That means no winds blow. Over billions of years, lots of rocks from space have crashed into Mercury. Each one left a hole, or crater, that still looks exactly as it did when it was formed.

Which planet is buried under thick clouds?

Venus. But the clouds are not like the clouds around Earth. Venus's clouds are bright yellow and they are poisonous. The planet is also the hottest planet of all. The 900 degree Fahrenheit (482 °C) temperature at its surface is hot enough to melt metal!

The sun shining on Venus makes the planet look very bright to us on Earth. Because it shows up just before sunrise or after sunset, people call Venus the "morning star" or the "evening star"—a name it got before anyone knew the difference between a star and a planet.

Why is Mars red?

Because the surface of Mars is covered with rocks that contain lots of iron. The iron has rusted. And as you know, rusted iron is red in color.

The surface of Mars is like a dry, rocky desert. In 1997 the *Pathfinder* spacecraft found that part of Mars was once flooded with water. Now the only water on the planet is frozen in ice caps around its North and South poles.

Which is the biggest planet?

Jupiter. The diameter of Jupiter is more than 10 times the diameter of Earth. More than 1,000 planets the size of Earth could fit inside Jupiter. A plane trip around Earth's equator would take about 40 hours. The same trip around Jupiter's equator would take 200 hours.

While Mercury, Venus, Earth, and Mars are mostly rock, Jupiter—as well as Saturn, Uranus, and Neptune— is mostly gas with some liquid. Only the central core is solid. And while Earth has 1 moon, Jupiter has 16 moons.

Which planet is known for its beautiful rings?

Saturn. Seven rings made of chunks of ice and rock revolve in orbit around the planet. The rings are very wide—but very flat. They are so thin that astronomers can see distant stars through them. Yet the rings are heavy enough to cast shadows on Saturn.

Saturn has 18 moons. That is more than any other planet in our solar system. The largest moon, Titan, is the only moon in our solar system with an atmosphere.

Which planet spins on its side?

Uranus. It rotates like the other planets. But this planet is tilted way over. It looks like a top spinning on its side.

Through a telescope we can see the rich blue-green color of Uranus. The color comes from gases in its atmosphere.

We can also see the 11 rings that astronomers found around Uranus in 1977. They are like the rings around Saturn but are less visible because they are made up of dark chunks of matter.

Which planet is usually eighth and sometimes ninth from the sun?

Neptune. As a rule, it is the eighth planet in the solar system. But every 248 years, Neptune swings out past Pluto. For about 20 years—most recently between the years 1979 and 1999—Neptune is the ninth planet from the sun. The rest of the time, it's back to eighth place.

Astronomers knew Neptune was there before they actually found it. There were signs that another planet was pulling on Uranus's orbit. The scientists looked around—and that's how they found Neptune.

Is Pluto really a planet?

Yes and no. A few astronomers call Pluto a comet, which is a small, cold body in space. Out beyond Pluto are lots of comets—and these scientists believe Pluto is just one of them. The surface temperature of Pluto is around −400 degrees Fahrenheit (−240 °C). And its size is smaller than Earth's moon.

Less is known about Pluto than any other planet because of its great distance from Earth. Pluto is never closer than almost 3 billion miles (4.8 billion km).

How long is a day on each planet? How long is a year?

A day is the time it takes a planet to rotate once. Earth takes 24 hours. Since each planet rotates at a different speed, the length of a day varies from planet to planet.

A year is the time it takes a planet to revolve once around the sun. Earth takes 365 days, or one Earth year. Since each planet is at a different distance from the sun and each travels at a different speed, the length of a year varies from planet to planet.

Here's how Earth compares to the other planets:

	Rotation (In Days/Hours)*	Revolution Around the Sun (In Days/Years)*
Mercury	59 days	88 days
Venus	243 days	225 days
Earth	24 hours	365 days
Mars	26 hours	687 days
Jupiter	10 hours	12 years
Saturn	10 hours	30 years
Uranus	17 hours	84 years
Neptune	18 hours	165 years
Pluto	6 days	248 years

*(Time is given in Earth days, Earth years, or hours.)

Do things weigh the same on all the planets?

It seems strange, but weight changes from planet to planet! Weight depends on the pull of gravity. And the bigger the planet, the stronger the pull of gravity.

Let's say you weigh 80 pounds (36 kg) on Earth. On Jupiter, the biggest planet, you would weigh more than 200 pounds (90 kg). On Pluto, the smallest planet, you would weigh only about ¹/₂ pound (224 g).

Are there other planets in the universe?

It sure looks that way! After all, the universe holds billions of stars. There's a good chance that at least some stars have planets, like our sun does.

In 1994, two astronomers found a star with three planets around it. The star is known as Pulsar 1257+12. It is more than 600 light-years from Earth. The three planets are respectively 19, 33, and 43 million miles (30, 53, and 69 million km) from the star.

Today, astronomers have very advanced telescopes. They use them to discover bodies beyond Pluto. Some of these bodies may prove to be planets.

OTHER OBJECTS IN SPACE

What is our closest neighbor in space?

The moon. It is much closer to Earth than any other body in space. The distance is less than 240,000 miles (384,000 km). Compare this to the sun at 93 million miles (149 million km)!

The moon is in orbit around Earth. A body that orbits a planet is called a moon, or natural satellite.

Why does the moon shine?

Because it bounces back, or reflects, light from the sun. Even when your part of Earth is dark, the sun lights up one side of the moon. The side of the moon turned away from the sun is always dark.

Why does the moon change its shape from night to night?

The moon only *seems* to change. It stays round. But our view changes as it orbits Earth.

On some nights the side of the moon facing Earth is not lit up by sunlight. We cannot see the moon. We call that a new moon.

Nights pass and we see only a small part of the moon. It looks like a thin, curved slice. We call this a crescent moon.

Night after night, we see more of the lighted side of the moon. It keeps getting rounder. We call these shapes first quarter and gibbous. Finally, the entire side of the moon facing Earth is lit. We call this a full moon.

During the following nights the moon grows smaller. Finally it's a new moon again. Almost a whole month has passed.

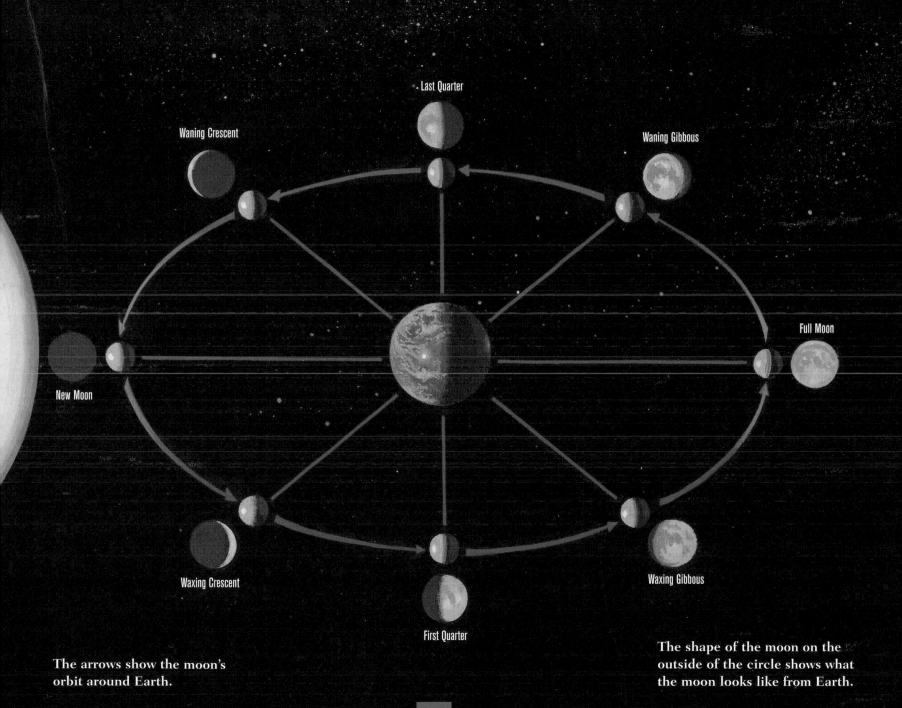

Last Quarter

Waning Crescent

Waning Gibbous

New Moon

Full Moon

Waxing Crescent

Waxing Gibbous

First Quarter

The arrows show the moon's
orbit around Earth.

The shape of the moon on the
outside of the circle shows what
the moon looks like from Earth.

What is "the man in the moon"?

Dark rocks on the moon that look like a face. The rocks are lava from volcanoes. Some lava also formed large, flat plains, called maria.

In and around the maria are billions of big and small holes, called craters. Craters are made by solid objects from space that crash into the moon. The craters have stayed the same for millions of years.

The light areas you see on the moon are a layer of grayish-brown soil. It is mostly ground-up bits of rock.

Is there life on the moon?

No, there is no life on the moon.

On July 20, 1969, astronaut Neil Armstrong became the first human to set foot on the moon. It took him about three days to make the rocket trip. After Armstrong, 11 more American astronauts landed on the moon.

They explored the surface. The soil held no sign of plant or animal life, past or present. The rocks they brought back had no chemicals produced by living beings. The photos they took showed no traces of life. The instruments they left on the moon tell the same story: The moon is a lifeless object in space.

Do other planets have moons?

Many do. Pluto matches Earth with 1 moon. Mars tops us with 2. Far greater in number are Neptune, with 8 moons; Jupiter, with 16; and Uranus, with 17. Saturn holds the record with 18 moons.

What is a comet?

A comet is a bright body that orbits the sun in an oval-shaped path. Some call comets "dirty snowballs" because they have icy centers with bits of rock and metal frozen inside.

About a million miles (1.6 million km) of gases and dust surround a comet's center. Together, the center and the gases and dust make up a comet's head.

A comet develops a bright gas-and-dust tail when it comes near the sun. The tail may be 100 million miles (160 million km) long. Sometimes it's easy to see a comet for several weeks before it moves away from Earth.

Some comets show up every few years. Others may pass near the sun only once in thousands or millions of years. Still others we never see because they are too far out in the solar system.

Why is Halley's comet famous?

Halley's (HAL-eez) comet is a very bright comet that appears about once every 76 years. It was first recorded in the year 240 B.C. You can look forward to seeing Halley's comet next around the year 2062.

The comet was named for Edmond Halley (1652–1742). He observed the comet in 1682 and compared it to many historical sightings. Based on this, he proposed that this comet returns regularly. Unfortunately, Halley died before 1758, the next time the comet returned.

What is an asteroid?

Some astronomers call asteroids "junk in the sky." But "minor planets" is a better name, since asteroids are really very small, rocky planets. Scientists know of about 30,000 asteroids. Many more exist, for sure.

Asteroids orbit the sun, just like planets. But most of them are found in a band or belt between Mars and Jupiter. This band is called the asteroid belt.

Which is the largest asteroid?

Ceres. It is about 600 miles (960 km) in diameter. Astronomers know its orbit so well that they can predict its location far in advance.

Ceres and the other asteroids were probably formed in much the same way as the major planets. They probably date back to the formation of the solar system.

Do asteroids ever strike Earth?

Sometimes. The gravity of a passing planet may pull an asteroid out of the asteroid belt. This can send it flying toward Earth. Usually, little or nothing happens. Most asteroids drop into the ocean or fall onto land without harming anyone.

Around 65 million years ago, a 9-mile-wide (14.4 km) asteroid crashed to Earth—and changed history. The asteroid exploded, flinging great amounts of dust and smoke into the atmosphere. Some think this blocked the sun's light for many months, killing all the plants. Without plants, the plant-eating dinosaurs starved to death. Then the dinosaurs who ate the plant eaters also died off.

We can't be sure that the asteroid killed off the dinosaurs. But there is little doubt that an asteroid hit Earth around the time the dinosaurs disappeared.

Will other asteroids strike Earth?

Astronomers know the orbits of about 4,000 asteroids. They look for any that might crash to Earth. Experts will see them long before they come close. If one looks dangerous, scientists will try to explode the asteroid in space.

What are meteoroids, meteors, and meteorites?

Meteoroids are chunks of rock or metal flying through space. They are much smaller than asteroids. Some are no larger than specks of dust.

Millions of meteoroids head toward Earth every day. As they pass through Earth's atmosphere, friction makes them white hot. They leave behind a trail of hot, glowing gases. This trail forms a streak of light in the sky called a meteor.

About 500 of these bodies reach Earth every year. Only a few fall on land. Those that are found on land are known as meteorites.

Is a "shooting star" a star?

No. A shooting star is a meteor. Long ago, people could not understand these streaks across the sky. They thought they were stars falling to Earth. But now we know they are nothing more than meteoroids flying through the atmosphere.

Is there life elsewhere in the solar system?

Scientists think so. In 1996, they noticed golden specks in a rock that had fallen to Earth from Mars. The specks are chemicals that may have come from tiny living things on Mars some three billion years ago. Then, in 1997, the *Pathfinder* spacecraft found volcanic rocks on Mars—another sign that life was possible.

Recently, too, scientists found conditions that may suggest life on the moons around Jupiter. And Europa, Io (EYE-oh), and Ganymede (GAN-uh-meed) are surrounded by magnetic fields, which could mean that they have hot cores. Both conditions, water and hot cores, seem to be necessary for life.

What questions are astronomers still asking?

Here are a few:

- How big is the universe?
- Are there planets orbiting other stars in space?
- Can humans live on Mars?
- Is there intelligent life anywhere else in the universe?

And there are many more. Astronomers are curious—just like you. They're always asking questions and looking for answers. Their answers usually lead to new questions. That's what being an astronomer is all about!

Index

About the Authors

Melvin and Gilda Berger live on a street where there are no lights or nearby houses. On clear nights, they can see the most brilliant skies. All year long, they stargaze and watch for meteors. "We feel lucky to have the greatest show on Earth above our rooftop," say the Bergers.

About the Illustrator

Vincent Di Fate was introduced to the wonders of space when he was four years old and went to his first science fiction movie. He was inspired to be an artist by the beautiful paintings of Chesley Bonestell. Mr. Bonestell studied stars and planets through a telescope before he painted them. Mr. Di Fate says, "The paintings took me to those far worlds and made me understand the power of art."